Pastorals

PASTORALS

by

Rachel Hadas

Measure Press
Savannah, Georgia

Printed in the United States of America
First Edition

The text of this book is composed in Baskerville.
Composition by R.G.
Manufacturing by Ingram.

Hadas, Rachel
Pastorals / by Rachel Hadas — 1st ed.

ISBN-13: 978-1-939574-39-8
ISBN-10: 1-939574-39-0
Library of Congress Control Number: 2025932803

Measure Press
2 Longberry Lane
Savannah, GA 31419
http://www.measurepress.com/measure/

For my father and mother, who bought the house; my husband, who shares it with me; my son, who will inherit it; and for the relatives and friends, neighbors and guests and ghosts, past, passing, and to come.

CONTENTS

Pastorals

Summer Variations I

Summer after summer rings changes on the theme of nostalgia—homesickness for what came before but is still present. Can one feel nostalgic for the present, especially when it's layered so palpably over the past? I still use some of the same pots and pans my mother used. Until recently I wore one of her nightgowns. A patch of yellow paint on the attic wall is what remains of the time this corner of the space was a bedroom (sheetrock partitions, long since gone, but the back wall remains) where my half-brother and his wife used to sleep. The answer to that question is: of course.

Talking around the table: gay witty banter, I dubbed this table talk for some reason while I was still a child. Another phrase from the Fifties floats back to me: I was commenting that the lettuce or spinach from the garden my mother had planted behind the house hadn't been washed, was gritty. And then I added "I like sand."

Seasonal phantoms reappear. Have they been dormant all winter every winter? Walter De La Mare's poem "The Listeners" describes ghosts so gently that when I read the poem as a child, I was unsure whether "the host of phantom listeners/That dwelt in the lone house then" were really ghosts. I was right to be puzzled; De La Mare's "phantoms" were and were not spirits of the dead. They weren't angry or aggressive; they were just attentive and possibly lonely. Hard to tell. Were they waiting for the traveler to leave, or did they miss him once he was gone? Once he'd ridden away, "the silence surged softly backward." We aren't told how the phantoms feel. We never know how the phantoms feel.

Ghosts: filmy and elusive. Harmless because invisible? Because invisible imaginary? Dismiss the phantoms and away they rustle, but only as far as that line of maples at the bottom of the valley, the trees whose runic leaves spell *immortality* until I put my distance glasses on and see it is *mortality* they spell out.

Invisible presences are palpable if not audible here, once the house is inhabited again. The house is silent in the winter, not the summer. But moments of silence occur in the summer too, indoors and outdoors, and that's when these presences are most likely to make themselves felt. I might be going up the stairs or walking to the compost heap or down the driveway to the mailbox, and be struck by—memory isn't as precise a word as presence. The presence of an absence. Or halfway up the hill in a tangle of blackberries, scratched and spotted with blood and juice, in humid silence, I might think I'm being watched. Something, someone is close by, attentive, listening.

Dream: The Summer House in Winter

Carrying little lambent green globes, my dead pace along quietly in their designated lane. A steep and muddy hill I don't remember having seen before rears up behind the house. It is a house of health and desolation, of healing and sickness. On a bench by the front door two women sit, passing a weeping girl child back and forth, one woman's lap to the other.

Behind the door, a staircase to a scrubbed attic full of books. *We knew for long the mansion's look/And what we said of it became/A part of what it is,"* wrote Wallace Stevens in "A Postcard from the Volcano." These loaded and bulging summer shelves also held food for winter. What but affection feeds the fire, once summer has subsided into memory?

The quiet dead keep walking, holding aloft their lamps, whose pale glow reaches out to the lane of the living—the living for a little while.

Summer Variations II

Of course, the stories of summer vary year by year. The summer of 1988 was hot and humid, and I mostly remember swinging in the hammock with my son, then five years old, and reading to him. In the summer of 1973, there were torrential rains; the roof of our neighbors' house slid into the brook. Rains again in 2011—Hurricane Irene—and again in 2023, when people were kayaking across State Street in Montpelier. Ovid and Lucretius both describe scenes that evoke those washed-out roads, floating trees, drowned animals. Nothing new. 2024: rain again, a year to the day after the floods of 2023. And then two weeks later. Again.

Summer dawns: year after year, the beds brim with dreams about past winters, struggles, travels, encounters. As a general rule, in the city I dream about the country and vice versa.

And reenactments sometimes deciphered long after the fact, understood in belated flashes: my mother on her knees weeding, or pacing slowly, almost drifting (like Mrs. Wilcox in *Howards End*, my friend Dick said once), trailing a few blades of grass or an uprooted weed in one hand. Have I become her? My weeding impulse often gives out once I've pulled up a few blades of grass. Or my father, sitting at a rickety table on the porch or in the barn, typing with two fingers—have I become him? Stavros building a stone wall and digging irrigation channels in the vegetable garden. George at the piano upstairs. Shalom in his studio, darkly shaded by the trees outside the window so that the room is ideally dim and the screen shines brightly. An earlier version of this room was my son's bedroom. Summer after summer, he and his best friend Ethan bounced on the bed so hard and high that the springs of the old bed (not new when my father and my half-brother David bought it at Penniman's junk store) collapsed. Earlier still, that same room used to be known as the French room because a travel poster nailed to the door showed a beaming blond boy on a ski slope somewhere in the French Alps. When David was sick with a streaming cold or something worse, the French room became his sick room. In the room where Shalom and I slept until we moved downstairs to my mother's old room, there used to be twin beds for my sister and me, with pink and rose and mauve striped bedspreads, a sort of Barbie touch more than half a century in advance. These beds were replaced by a wooden double bed constructed by my brother's first wife, who enjoyed carpentry. In time that bed was relegated to the attic, and we bought a double bed. "The careful monks patch and patch it," wrote Keats, "till not a thread of the original fabric is left, but still they show it for St. Stephen's shirt." And so with this house. With families.

Dream: Mothers and Sons

A dingy farmhouse on a back road. On the upper floor, many small bedrooms. All their doors are shut; none is locked. In every room a double bed, a tumbled quilt, walls of no color, day leaking in through threadbare curtains. In each bed, asleep, at any rate not awake, a mother and a son lie intertwined. The mothers—I can see this at a glance, however weak the light and partial my view from the threshold—are more or less my age: not young. The sons, grown up, had all gone far away and have evidently now returned home, if only long enough to eat supper and go upstairs to sleep in their childhood rooms.

No fathers.

The faces are illegible in sleep: attentive, focused, blank, thoughtful, all or none of these. Perhaps each mother-son dyad is dreaming of the journeys that beached them there together, bed by bed, if only for one night, warm and tangled in the breathing sheets. Or maybe each mother shares her dream with all the other mothers, each son with all the other sons.

I tiptoe back down the stairs.

Dream: The Pink and White Wallpaper

In what dream witchery did you extract from the pink and white flowered wallpaper a single spray, transformed to three dimensions, the tiny hairs still clinging to its root, and then courteously hand this plant to me? Mere gallantry—a corsage, a bouquet? Or some unspoken intention for me to infer?

And there was more. A woman glimpsed through a half-opened door, making her bed. The sheets were apple green. Somewhere in this room was a big blank screen you brushed against; and by some trick of optics or sleight of hand, the figures locked in flatness behind the glass took on heft and shape before my eyes, became suddenly three-dimensional, like the plant.

The Old House

The old house a Pandora's box of needs.

She glanced up from her book and met my eyes. We smiled and shook our heads.

"I come to life," she says, "when you are here. Year after year, a lingering last look and a promise. Live in me, animate me, keep me warm. Who but you can fill my empty spaces?"

Starting slowly, speeding up, days cluster and accumulate. The house: is it a big kaleidoscope? An anchor? Or a threadbare procession of passing pilgrims whose hope of a mild interlude in a green zone yields to the need to wake and dress and leave, once they have put their city faces on?

In Secondhand Prose, St. Johnsbury's secondhand bookstore, where I buy too many poetry anthologies year after year, I found and have since lost a poem by John Ashbery that contains the line "silence already filled with noise." I can't think of a better description of these summers—or wait, "noise already filled with silence" works just as well. Benign silences of people's individual lives, the rhythms of different days, the interlude here. No master list exists of all the guest who've come over the years, but their friendly phantoms hang around. When Alicia Stallings, exhausted between the end of one writer's conference and the beginning of another, visited in 2019, the whooshing of the dryer in the room behind the bedroom where she was resting and the buzzing of bees audible on the porch outside combined to lull her into the first nap she'd taken in years.

Outside the room, life went on. None of the doors in the house shuts tight, a feature it shares with our (also old) New York apartment. Life as background noise? Dreams the foreground?

Windows, Doors

Each window in this house faces in a different direction and therefore frames a different view. Not only that; seasons and weather have to be factored in: sun, snow, cloud, smoke from wildfires. Rain drumming on the roof. Misty mornings. Deciduous trees and evergreens alike tossed by wind. A few birds busy in the branches of the hemlock tree we can see from our downstairs bedroom window—the tree that keeps the room dark.

Apply the time of day, the way the light falls. Then fold in mood and memory, guests and ghosts, generations passing through each room, sleeping in the bedrooms, waking up and looking out the window.

Don't forget the phases of the moon. Some nights the moon shines in the window. The hills outside are silver-grey with black shadows. On clear nights when it isn't overwhelmed by moonlight, the Big Dipper rides above the barn.

Seen from outside while the lights are still on at night, the house looks cheerful and inviting. When we turn off the lights, the frames fill up with images and scraps of story retrieved from individual inner sources. You dream and then you wake up, open your eyes, take stock, sit up, stand up, and walk over to whichever window it is that frames the weather of another morning.

And so many doors in this house. Door/gate/portal, open/closed. Inside and outside meet. One room becomes another room. The threshold is a boundary that throbs with meaning but also is inconspicuous enough to be almost invisible until you look back and understand that you have crossed from one realm to another, with maybe one last glance over your shoulder at the baffled revenant, travel-stained, weary, waiting on the other side to be let in.

The Fourth of July

It feels like, though it isn't, the midpoint of summer. Horizontal light picks out a fly in a dusty web; mouse droppings fresh on my desk each morning; poem drafts; letters. A bee, stunned or sunning, lies on the sill. On the walls: the water lily poster; photo of my father; NO TRESPASSING sign acquired how and when I don't remember. Emblems, emblems.

Flip a coin. In Greek, *korona/grammata*: crown/letters. Heads or tails sounds spermy. Or pull petals from flowers, the destructive divination from childhood: *he loves me, he loves me not.* Then the bald unwinking sun-eyed daisy is discarded.

July fourth. When it finally gets dark, red and green and orange fireworks drown out the silent moonlight. After the American flag in lights at the ends of the show, a little voice is heard to ask: "Was that all?" In the dark, barefoot children draped in their parents' sweaters stagger around on wet grass.

Big, also barefoot, a few days later I step too close to a small snake in the road, assuming it's dead. It gathers its little body and raises its head and makes as if to strike, then slithers off into the brush at the side of the road. And here's another snake. This one seems to be curled up asleep in the dusty ditch; but as I bend to look more closely, I can see its guts leaking out of its side. The restful posture is death.

The barn whose roof caved in after the fierce blizzard last spring gapes at the sky: majestic, half-ruined, stoical, waiting to be repaired, or maybe to be abandoned, and in that case slowly sinking down onto its Cyclopean foundation stones, boulders which oxen must have hauled to this spot more than a century ago.

Summer Weather

This afternoon the brimming trough of water in the meadow offers no more or less news than the steady sky it matches. Both are pewter-colored, gleaming; both tilted, watchful, sly as a mirror.

The sky and the hour deepen, and the water shrugs in its clouded coat. In the stillness, a muted rhythm (woodpecker knocking?) taps somewhere unseen. The light fades to blank.

A slight unease prevails, an interlude where the unknowable ripples and shivers. How long the sky will frown, whether it will rain, there's no telling until it happens. Then muffled adjustments, readjustments, and the sun breaks out of an impasse and shines—no, beats down.

Would I forget you, hillside, trough brimming with water that never stays the same color?

Abeyance doesn't mean I won't return.

Meadow

Often, wrote Robert Duncan, *I am permitted to return to a meadow as if it were a scene made up by the mind, that is not mine, but a made place, that is mine, it is so near to the heart, an eternal pasture folded in all thought.*

Through the foam of Queen Anne's Lace, knee-deep, I walk toward where the maple sentinels are standing and the woods begin to darken. The field divides itself into little slopes. Wind combs the grasses. An achieved emptiness; a protection. Wildflowers. Silence.

Often I am permitted to return to a meadow as if it were a given property of the mind that certain bounds hold against chaos.

The meadow is not mine. *It is only a dream of grass blowing east against the source of the sun in an hour before the sun's going down*

Morning and evening the meadow is a cover and a memory, vulnerable and tough, placid and expressive, eternal, old, and new. There was a rock that for years I used to climb and perch on and look down over the meadow slanting below and take stock. There was a rock, and there still is, but now the rock is screened, the view mantled, by young trees.

Sightlines; privacy; the lattice work of leaves. The return. What changes and does not change.

A place of first permission, everlasting omen of what is

Everlasting if we are vigilant. If we are lucky. If we manage to hold to the place and also to pass it on, we may be permitted to return.

Hum of the Season

Stretched out on the sofa after lunch, I'm marginally aware of a woman's voice on the radio crisply holding forth on the sex lives of insects. At a woolly distance, I take in that the male honeybee has evolved a scoop-like apparatus on the tip of his penis to facilitate the removal of any phallic fragments his predecessor may have left behind. Male honeybees when they ejaculate, she adds, explode.

Voices before sleep fade. Hers is sinking to a hum, as of a mosquito cruising the sultry afternoon. I get up and go out and walk across the lawn.

Hum of the season and of the surround. Bees in the bee balm; also hummingbirds, which go, says Ishmael Reed, straight for the eyes. Bees in the towering top-heavy snake root, which is also called Black Cohosh, although its fragrant, spiky flowers are white. White flower, black root—like moly?

I wander around to the back of the house, which some people call the front. Between house and barn is a flourishing chestnut oak tree. Possibly first constructed by some other bird now gone—eggs hatched, fledglings flown—the robin's nest in the chestnut oak is empty. Long strands of dead grass hang down from the nest—dolefully, I want to say, wallowing in the pathetic fallacy. Or just hang there like wisps of hair that have come astray.

That tree where the empty nest is precariously balanced—wedged?—between two branches: family tradition has it that my mother planted a sprouting acorn that she found in Central Park (or was it Riverside Park?) and brought up here. Family tradition, oral tradition, urban/rural legend, anecdote and memory both blurred and burnished. My book-loving family were never very interested in keeping records.

Bees in the bee balm. The hummingbirds zoom back and forth.

From my perch on the screened porch, I have a good view of the phoebe family —both outside on the lawn and inside, where I'm sitting at a battered white enamel table. Out on the lawn, the mother phoebe flips her tail up and down, up and down, as she perches on the back of a lawn chair and then hops to another and then another. We've been leaving the door to the screened porch open, so Mrs. Phoebe can also perch on top of the door on her way to the nest. From that height she swoops and ducks and flies in and out all day. Another point of entrance is the narrow space between the screened windows and the porch floor, left there by a builder for some reason it's now hard to fathom, unless he was thinking of avian convenience. (Also, it occurs to me, he was the husband of one of my mother's best friends.). Mrs. Phoebe knows how to fly through that tight space—another way in and out.

Her eggs, in the nest she has built in an angle where the porch wall meets the ceiling, have hatched by now. I can hear the soft chirping of the nestlings, and if I stand back and crane my neck, I can just catch a glimpse of their gaping little beaks as she swoops swiftly in to feed them I'm not sure what. Then, since she no longer needs to sit in her nest (there's no room for her in any case, on top of four rapidly growing baby birds), she's off again.

On the table where I sit and look out through the screen at the garden, the table where I write and where I sometimes make collages:

phoebe poop. (The table is directly below the new nest.). Down the backs of the lawn chairs: phoebe poop. On the floorboards of the porch; on the ratty quilt that covers the cot at the far end of the porch: phoebe poop. And a new development: on the floor of the barn, like an unwelcome visitor from the city, pigeon poop. We never used to have pigeons in the barn—just phoebes and barn swallows—or not until last fall. The particularly viscous, adhesive texture of pigeon poop was something I'd always associated with New York City windowsills and awnings, but now hardened piles of the stuff formed little mounds on the barn floor. Our neighbor and his stepson eventually pressure-washed that floor. The porch, with its softer and fresher phoebe droppings, was something I could and did deal with daily.

Indoors, tiny ants are crawling over the kitchen counter. Trying to keep such surfaces wholly free of anything greasy or sweet is a quixotic enterprise, a battle that can't be won.

All of this has been done before; it will all need redoing. The clean-up in life is constant. When we stop needing to mop up after those who came before us, or to make room for those who will follow, is when we abandon the cycle.

But not yet. The barn with its stalactites of pigeon excrement defeats me, but I'm going back into the kitchen now. I'll ignore the ants and fish a bottle of Simple Green out from under the sink. A roll of paper towels is on the enamel porch table already. I'll spray and scrub, and the table will be briefly pristine for whatever it will next host as I sit there and look out at the garden and down the vistas of past summers. I'll wipe up what by now must be almost the last of this generation's leavings; soon the fledglings will venture out of the nest and flutter and stagger around the porch. I can hardly bear to watch that stage, but the cats are safely indoors, probably asleep upstairs. The cycle goes on.

The phoebe whose drab color matches the brown and grey of the faded lawn chairs is probably a descendant of the phoebe that built a nest on this same porch one summer late in my father's life, perhaps even his last summer. She is also, presumably, a closer descendant of the phoebe that built her nest on this porch one of those years during the pandemic when we arrived before spring had begun and stayed on until almost the end of November. Each year the phoebes' nest in a different spot somewhere among the rafters of the porch. The nests built in previous summers remain, still sturdy so far as one can tell, but as empty as unrented summer cottages. Traditionalists who also relish variety, each generation of phoebes builds a new nest regardless.

Theme with variations? James Merrill's poem "Another August," whose title fits these reflections of mine, would, if I understand it, delete variation: "Open the shutters. Let variation/abandon the swallows one by one./How many summer dusks were needed/to make that single skimming form!/The very firefly kindles to its type." Summer after summer carves and molds the archetypal shape into the most streamlined, economical version of itself. Lines adapted, scenes reset: resurrected recurrences we recognize, reenact, forget, reenact again.

Walking around the Triangle: Sermon in Stone

The fern, the moss, the shadow, and the stone. The shadow of the fern on a stone green with moss slowed me, then stopped me. So begin again. Stone; moss (bright green; velvet-soft); fern; shadow; sun. *A violet by a mossy stone*—not quite, but in the dappled foliage of the memory, not far, either. Ground beneath my feet. *Sermons in stones and good in everything.* In this stone. I find a rock to sit on, and I gaze.

An hour is a year, the poet Chard deNiord said yesterday. He also said *Today's tomorrow:* lesson daily, hourly learned.

Afternoon is nothing but itself. *In the afternoon they came unto a land/In which it seemed always afternoon.* It was afternoon when Jane Hirschfield read from her poems upstairs in the St. Johnsbury Athenaeum. To be almost blinded by the westering sun slanting through the tall windows behind Jane felt exalted, hushed and saturated as stained glass. That reading happened to take place upstairs only because the gallery downstairs was undergoing some sort of renovation to nudge it forward from 1873. But downstairs we wouldn't have been able to see that shaft of sun.

Hard to make out behind that stand of pine trees, the westering sun here imprints a perfect shadow of fern on stone. Time yields to space, if you obey the call and find a log and sit and—no more verbs.

Stone. Moss. Fern. Shadow. Sun. The fern's facsimile in the shadow's shape slowed, then stopped me. Where had I been going? Around the triangle, as we used to call it: a loop around three roads, one less a road these past ten years than a track, *because it was grassy and wanted wear,* ever since Hurricane Irene swept through and washed that part of Brook Road out. The road crew never fixed it and maybe never will. With minor detours, it's still walkable. But the Town of Danville has put concrete barriers at either end of the road: CLASS 4 ROAD. PROCEED AT YOUR OWN RISK. Or words to that effect.

I looped back toward home. Home, away; home—the story. *The way up and the way down are one and the same. There would still remain the never-resting mind,* parsing the shadow of a fern on stone.

Walking around the Triangle: Spiderwebs

I saw two spiderwebs meet in midair above the brook. Sitting on a stone, bare feet in icy water, I wasn't anticipating anything, just listening to the sound of rushing water. Light slanted through the trees on the far bank. Attached to adjacent branches that seemed to reach out to each other in space, but angled a bit away from each other, the two webs were suspended over the brown and white babble and bubble. Just perceptibly, they trembled.

Each had a tiny spider at its heart.

Would the webs still be intact the next day? I meant to go back and see. But as it does, life nudged me away from the quiet in which I'd be able to study the two webs, twin systems kissing lightly in midair.

Walking around the Triangle: The Doherty Place

The house—I pass it walking home—is closed. The family have left. Maybe they'll be back for Labor Day. There's hardly any wind, yet the wind chimes on the porch tinkle discreetly. Two worn flags, nearly translucent as the light pours through them, quietly strain on their pole. US and Ireland? Ireland and Vermont? I've already forgotten. High overhead, a tiny plane draws a line between the rising moon and the setting sun.

I sit down on the stone bench next to the flagpole. As if someone had just now gotten up, the swing suspended from a tall pine on the patch of lawn sloping down to the Water Andric sways slightly. There's nobody home. The bench is granite, neither cool nor warm.

Walking around the Triangle: Widow Road

Whose is that shadow in the hayfield—the meadow that, in the days when someone still mowed it, was a front lawn? Through a window: a cluttered room—a room empty of people. It's possible to make out part of a piano, the corner of a table.

Outside, tall grass. A tennis ball. A rawhide bone. Pinecones. Windfall apples. A picnic table knee-deep in ferns. A half-collapsed hibachi. Suspended from a tall pine, a swing sways in the wind.

The gaping barn.

Lost in a Living Maze

A slab of clarity carved out of cloud. A spiral staircase winding up and disappearing into mist. A door—and who has the key? *In the midst of a lockdown, I am lost in a living maze,* wrote a British poet, Tristram Fane Saunders.

Lost, lost. My son can't find his birth certificate, which he needs to replace his passport (also lost). To go where?

I recognized the roads, but I was having trouble keeping up. "Wait!" I called hoarsely. The ones in front turned back to look at me, then turned away again and kept on climbing.

Tall locked door, frosted glass: I stood on tiptoe trying to peer in. No lights. No one was there.

To try to impose a pattern on the pottage and porridge of daily confusion: the daily round, the soft, the hard, steel girders folded in and out of cloud, intermittently visible this mild afternoon, the moon waxing and days getting longer.

Where can we find a place to stand? Groping through memory won't get us there, wherever there is. Where did we want to go? *Be present* is a predictable instruction. Less often said: how slyly and how fast the present glides out of sight and hides somewhere behind us. If we were in the country now, we would enter the labyrinth and follow its curves, and look up and touch the rough or smooth bark of bare trees in passing, and then look down: dead leaves and pinecones poking through traces of snow. In the absence of a labyrinth, only a straight path from here to there.

The lostness is its own mode of escape. We would trudge down the road, down the winding hill toward the sound of running water. The thaw would have arrived. As it got warmer, we would hang our coats on a branch and keep on moving. Slow, enormous changes invisible till now would become apparent—had already become apparent, but we seem to need to pass through the maze over and over to become aware of them. A spiral staircase winds up and vanishes in mist. One radiant slit of light is carved out of cloud.

Those Flannel Nightshirts

So far the nights feel lonelier than the days. In the daytime, the living keep me company—that, and years' worth of remembered voices. Each summer threads a familiar maze. Emerging into a new morning, day, year, you barely notice the slow kaleidoscope of clouds and hours. And it turns.

Those flannel nightshirts chilly sleepers wear as summer wanes—I'm giving them away to my son's friends. Passing it on—a way of keeping it at the same time. The red plaid tunics make them look like members of the same team.

A bough has broken off from the Duchess tree. Rain swelled the apples, or maybe the French-Canadian pruner was too enthusiastic. Too much lightness weighs heavy: the heft of the idea of home, tempered with the detachment and passivity of a dream, and swaying with an undertow of tidal pulls, like the ocean, like sunrise.

Star and Sweater, Cat and Moon

Though the years are sometimes blurry, the seasons are as reliable as phases of the moon. Still, I can get confused. Last night I ventured out, drawn by a patch of intense brightness in the sky—the new moon, so I thought, partly obscured (it must have been October or November) by the branches of a leafless tree. But it was not the moon, which rose and set on schedule a little later in a completely different part of the sky, above the slope behind the house. It was a star. The evening star? It was a planet—Venus? Jupiter?—big and brilliant. How could I have thought it was the moon?

Each time I glance at my grey ribbed wool sweater slung over the back of the sofa, I mistake it for our grey striped cat. And this mistake I keep making over and over all day, each time I happen to glance toward that corner of the room. My ability to absorb new information is stiffening, its agility is shot. My power to recognize what's in front of my nose, be it a sweater or the evening star, is fading, as the same set of stale assumptions slots as predictably into place as (to use the simile in George Orwell's "Politics and the English Language") cavalry horses answering the bugle. Orwell used this vivid though now dated simile to evoke the dreary predictability of dead metaphors; elsewhere in this essay he compares stale phrases and tropes choking a writer's mind to tea leaves blocking a sink.

Something is blocking something. I make excuses to myself. Planet, moon: both bright in a dark sky. Sweater, cat: both furry, grey, both conforming to the shape of the sofa. Not until I gather my resolve and remove my sweater from the sofa can I correct the stubborn error—am I convinced that it is my grey sweater and not the tiger cat.

Dream: Blackberries in Snow

In the thin light before dawn I've been padding around the room. Now I climb back into bed. I must have gone back to sleep: I wake up, or dream that I wake up, on a hill, the ridge where the neighbors' newish house is awkwardly perched. Deep snow all around, but the whiteness is punctuated by sprays of dead-ripe blackberries. No, I must be dreaming. These berries, glossy and unseasonable, are surely not a natural possibility in winter—though these days, who knows?

It's full daylight by now. The sheer contrast of black and white sheds its oddity and fits smoothly into my unfolding day; is forgotten. Only when darkness is returning do I think to ask: what did those berries mean? And that steep hill I struggled up through snow?

Question and Answer

One season raises questions. Dark December dawn: a shining presence stands in the threshold of the seminar room, signaling *It is time to cross the line.* Which line? Which threshold?

Another season answers. Wet weight of old snow dwindles to reveal last fall's leaves gleaming in the melt. A patch of ice dissolves in April sun. I open my eyes to daylight: brown earth, steaming, ready to be planted.

On My Knees: Morning Messengers

Not an epiphany, a revelation, any abrupt realization. It was more like a three-part feature film, a triple memory of a buried problem. Three buried problems.

I was kneeling planting onion sets one radiant June morning. Suddenly out of nowhere a line from a Shakespeare sonnet I hadn't been thinking about, hadn't read recently, hadn't known I knew, announced itself: *The other two, slight air and purging fire*...Sonnet 45 (I checked later). Air and fire? The other two? Sure enough, Sonnet 44 is about earth and water. I had recently written about fire and water, but that didn't seem to be the connection. *The other two:* a continuous chain of reference, a conversation caught in mid-air, or if not a conversation, then a monologue, a love letter, a meditation. Who are poets talking to, anyway?

My hands were still busy in the earth, but my mind slid away from the elements to a matter closer to home, more urgent—even if also impossibly distant—in the sparkling morning: who are you down there on your knees, wrist-deep in dirt, lines of poems skimbling through your head at random—or not at random? *Skimbling*: from T.S. Eliot's poem about Skimbleshanks the railway cat, whose nickname is Skimble. But I like *skimble* as a verb denoting a kind of nimble skittering, sliding, skipping.

Who are you? I asked myself. And then, so many decades after the fact: are you more your mother or your father? Neither. Both. They're long dead. But evidently it isn't only the memories of family faces that skip or skimble over decades; it's the flow of a mind. A memory for poems, for example, or for decontextualized snippets of poems.

Theodore Kitaif has written about memory that "images from our past are quietly but incessantly bubbling below the surface of consciousness, prepared to leap into the light…." But "have they come haphazardly, or with an indecipherable purpose that eludes the 'I' in whom they may have abided for years before appearing?" I can't answer that question, which hardly expects an answer anyway. But in my case, it's less images from the past than lines of poetry.

Back to my parents: I carry them in me, with me. First one predominates, and then the other. I cook. I try impatiently to garden. I sit at a table and write. All this I've known for years; it gets clearer with time, and also it doesn't. A small cycle: planting onion sets. A bigger cycle: the approach of limits.

I finished the rows of onions just barely poking their green tips out of the earth, and creakily stood up and stretched. A pang: my back was stiff, but that wasn't the source of the pang. No: I'd suddenly remembered that there was a letter I needed to write, and soon, to pull out of something to which I'd thoughtlessly agreed—a misstep, and I needed to step back; a mistake I needed to correct now, today. I went inside, washed the dirt off my hands, and sat down to write my recantation.

And yes, I was apprehensive—had been apprehensive while I was still out in the raw brown garden—that an angry, accusatory response would answer my withdrawal. No matter; I had to withdraw, and I did. And in fact, no such letter came; rather, a friendly answer. Maybe they'd expected all along that I'd pull out.

That afternoon, swaying in the hammock for a little while, I found myself staring at a lilac bush, burgeoning, purple—up here the lilacs often bloom as late as June. The flowers' fragrance floated toward me, suspended out of time in the sweet air. I kept on looking at the lilac bush: a yellow butterfly was tasting nectar, spray after luscious spray, in silence.

I climbed out of the hammock and reentered the day, but not before I recognized the messenger.

Dream: On My Knees

Down on my knees, I'm scrubbing armloads of grimy garments in a tub. Or am I kneeling to pick olives where they've fallen in the sparse grass of a Samian hillside? The washerwoman and the harvester—both editors of a sort? This is what it is to live in time, to remember what we can no longer feel, to feel what we no longer can remember. And then it bubbles up.

Endless Other Questions

I have been struggling to read a book I'd forgotten my father wrote—possibly not his best book, but nevertheless a book I need to read. A book from 1960. He was sixty. Did he know he had six more years to live?

Even if an answer were available, that's the wrong question. Though come to think of it, our financial advisor asked us just the other day, *How long do you think you'll live?* So maybe in the nearly sixty years since my father's death, the wrong question has become, if not the right question, then at least a standard question.

I wish I'd asked my father more questions—not actuarial questions but endless other questions. I want to reach out and back over the years, to somehow stretch across the strumming silence and say "I think maybe I know. I'm in that territory now. How was it for you? How did you manage it?" If he answered me, we might be able to compare notes. But mostly I hope I'd want to stay quiet, if I could do that—stay quiet and listen.

The glimpses I get are serendipitous, triangulated, sparse, tantalizing. I cherish them; they collapse the distance. Robert Pinsky writes in *Jersey Breaks* "In a certain kind of place, everything can feel simultaneous." Place; time.

Here's a nugget that came to me in a circuitous, contingent way—as if all our news from the past, and from the present for that matter, didn't arrive by a twisty route. Fresh out of Harvard, new to the metropolis where he'd always dreamed of living, and disappointed in whatever he was studying at Columbia's School of General Studies, John Ashbery enrolled in what turned out to be—as he described it in a letter—a transformational course: Greek Drama, taught by Moses Hadas.

Transformative how, precisely? My source, Rachel Trousdale's book about humor in American poetry, doesn't specify, though the quote does convey the young poet's excitement. That was the spring of 1950. John Ashbery was twenty-three. My father was pushing fifty. I was one and a half. The three of us at that time weren't all yet acquainted, but we have since achieved simultaneity. Greek drama, older than any of us, was always simultaneous. And is.

Draw a Picture of the *Iliad*

A year since I taught my last class. I tell myself and other people that I don't miss teaching, and it's mostly surprisingly true. And yet.

Sometime before the pandemic, I was inspired, or I was lazy enough, to ask the students in my mythology class to draw a picture of the *Iliad*. And as has always been my way, instead of taking pictures of the resulting sketches, I tried to describe a few of them in words.

Elisa's *Iliad*: the spectral face of Helen, floating above and behind the walls, takes up a corner of the page—no, spreads out to fill the entire sky. Helen (she isn't labelled, but it has to be Helen—or does it?) looks down from this vantage point at the chaos she has caused. Or has she? Was the war her fault? Facts have no place here. Her expression is hard to decipher.

Madani's *Iliad*: the Greek camp, schematic, tidy triangles of tents, the beach, the watch fires, no-man's-land, the walls and towers on the hill, all strategically mapped out and neatly depicted. He has filled his page from top to bottom. No named figures are in sight. As far as I can tell, no figures are visible.

Iqra's *Iliad*: Hector, Andromache, the nurse, the baby. No soldiers, ships, or walls.

Natalie's *Iliad*: Astyanax is crying. As he lies in his nurse's arms, we can see the tears spurting out of his eyes. Does the child know, does Natalie know, what good reason he has to cry?

Nolan's *Iliad*: a video game. At the top left-hand corner, we can see Mount Olympus; on the top right, an angry Zeus, fists bristling with thunderbolts. In the center, Achilles in full war gear, with carefully rendered helmet, breastplate, greaves. Hector is down somewhere at the bottom of the page. A woman and a child are huddled in one corner. No Helen.

None of these versions is right, none of them is wrong. None of them is complete. There is no way to include everything; even the *Iliad* includes by leaving out.

That floating face; the sensibility behind, above it all: eyebrows, cheekbones, a disembodied head. In *Mythistorema,* Seferis wrote:

> I woke with this marble head in my hands;
> it exhausts my elbows and I don't know where to put it down.
> It was falling into the dream as I was coming out of the dream
> so our life became one and it will be very difficult
> for it to separate again.

The battlefield the sea the sand the ships the fires the towers the walls the dust nights mornings the gods and yes, the mortals.

The human cost: incalculable, impossible to depict; and yet the sketches of the women and the baby tell a story we all know, a story of which we are reminded many times a day.

Pedagogy: I think I dreamed that one student became an expert on each topic and moved from group to group in a crowded room, explaining. Or was this not a dream? Why shouldn't it be true?

Not a lesson, I repeat over and over to what now feel like generations of students. Not a lesson but a vision.

Iqra. Nolan. Natalie. Madani. Elisa.

Multiply.

Blue Book

The blue book is light. As poetry can, it floats us beyond our sight, beyond the everyday. Riding the waves, we're carried out to sea. Or is it poetry that rides the waves? And also is the waves? Poetry is also the boat ("And love's the burning boy," says Elizabeth Bishop), rocking up and down, and we recline. "I am borne darkly, fearfully afar" is how Shelley puts it in *Adonais.* But not always fearfully and not always darkly. In the blue book, the blue boat, I lie back, lightly, lightly. The waves do all the work, they carry me, the breezes brush my hair.

What do we read? What do we need?

The poem knows more than we do; knows even when we do not. The poem picks us up and carries us away.

The blue book has dark depths, but is also light, perilous, playful as a foamy wave, but not without an undertow. The blue book is an odyssey. Is in fact *the* Odyssey: new islands, new harbors, new towns visited, as Tennyson and Cavafy and how many others retraced the scheme. The tour can even include the realm of the dead.

And at every pit stop, hospitality. Welcome, stranger! See how we live here. Bathe and eat and only then tell your tale; and before you leave, accept a parting gift to take with you for friendship's sake—guest friendship. In exchange, you gave us your journey this far, your storms, your war, your stories from before; and a promise of hospitality in the future.

Before we go, what do we need to know?

To lie back and remember that it wasn't always this way. Wasn't; will not be. We were elsewhere; we travelled back and forth, here and there. Now mostly here. Now only here. Now here: nowhere.

I have travelled, wrote Thoreau, a good deal in Concord. Just so.

Red Book

The red book is a stout biography, the kind that used to be called a doorstopper. Its title is *Red Comet*, but the book itself is more like a long freight train, a slow train, a train crammed with information, a train that stops at every station, not to let anyone out but to take more in. Not more passengers, but more records of three decades' worth of acts and facts: the precocious child, the college student, the dorm room with its yellow walls and dark green bedspread, courses taken, books read, notebooks filled, scrapbooks, drafts, papers, letters, dates. Days snatched in fragments and trapped on the page: aspiration; rage.

Or say it is a comet, not a train. The trail this comet made was, as is the nature of comets, bright and brief: an ardent arc of thirty years of a life, emblazoned across the middle of the twentieth century. She lived, she wrote, she married, she had two children, she struggled and strained against the cage of what *Red Comet* keeps reminding me was more than just a tightly girdled, was for woman a suffocating age. She died at thirty. She left a trail of poems.

Doomed? Not necessarily. Beginning, middle, end: a comet in its flight. And the biographer, after arduous research, sits down to write, to trace the arc and shape a narrative young woman poets read and recognize some parts of and wonder how to live.

Dream: The Quest

Scrambling down gullies, fording icy streams, staggering over snow-crust that keeps breaking, so that I keep sinking in up to my thighs and then pulling a sodden leg out again, first one leg, then the other, barely moving forward, pursued, pursuing, which is which, I stumble to a hut at the edge of a forest. Here a band of merciful young outlaws shelters me, gives me dry boots, a blanket, feeds me, lets me rest by their fire.

I mustn't sleep. I must be on my way. The darkness is unyielding, and the cold. Out again, among the trees: the tangle of black branches. Lantern light on snow. A friendly little square of fire-lit window behind me, but again I am pursued, pursuing: quest, flight, exile.

Dawn. Pale sky. Black boulders line the road. Between suddenly steep banks, a brackish stream is trickling downhill, toward a world underneath this one.

Inward, Outward

For the first half of life, we look inward; the second half, we look out, the poet Novalis is said to have opined. I can't remember where I read this, but I remember that these words stopped me. They still do.

Is the dictum true? Novalis lived from 1772 to 1801. The first half of his life was up to the age of fourteen. Having spent those fourteen years looking inward, did he then pivot, as we now might say, and look outward for his remaining years, all fourteen of them?

He died at twenty-eight. The girl he fell in love with, Sophie von Kuhn, was what, twelve years old when they met? Sophie died at sixteen. Which way, during her truncated life, was she looking? Surely near the end outward, toward her astonishing fiancé.

Couldn't a case be made that we begin by looking out, and only past life's midpoint, whenever that may be, turn our attention inward? Of course, both ideas are true, and they alternate. People vary. And yet I'm beginning to see what Novalis may have meant, when I think of my own relentless self-absorption. It has taken a long life (and maybe my life will be longer than seventy-five years) to learn to pay attention to the world around me. Curiosity is a muscle that needs to be developed and exercised. Could that be part of what Novalis had in mind? And what of his near-contemporary, Keats? Didn't he always look inward and out? And when Hamlet refers to humanity's "large discourse,/looking before and after," one thinks of time, but maybe also of space—inside, outside.

I'd like to poll my friends, eight women here at lunch, laughing around the table: where are you now in life? What portion do you see this summer day—in front of you? behind you? just right here? Most of us are well along toward our final destination. Does that mean, Alice, Barb, Bridget, Cindy, Elinor, Kris, Maddy, Reeve—does that mean that we are all now looking outside ourselves? Well, yes, we are. But inside as well. And whichever way each of us turns our gaze, what greets her eyes? What landscape of achievement or regret, of bliss and fear? What surprise?

Walk with Elephants

Late summer morning, mist not yet burned off. I and my neighbors on either side, Janet and Sharon, climb the hill on our weekly walk. Each of us carries her own silent elephant.

If my elephant, say, were somehow to drop from my back and plod and sway majestically away, knee-deep through the meadow frothy with Queen Anne's Lace and on toward that somber stand of maples, what would I say? What, straightening our backs, would any of us, once relieved of our burden, say?

That still unfinished cabin, that chained hound daily baying—these are not merely scenery we pass. They're also where we live. Take my house: it has a new red roof, but inside something's missing. Something is always missing. And something else is present and abundant.

Autumn is just around the corner. Dew-spangled cobwebs catch the morning light. Never free of elephants, one incomplete world blends into the next, glistening like this morning once the mist has burned off.

The Family Face

My niece is visiting—my half-brother David's daughter Debbie. David, who died in 2004, was eighteen years older than I am; Debbie is four years younger. With her parents and her brother, the four of them somehow all crammed into the attic to sleep, she spent summers in this house until she was maybe twelve or so. My parents, sister, and I took up the rest of the space.

Debbie is showing me recent pictures of her son Seth on her phone. Leaning in for a closer look, I peer at my great-nephew's face. He's in his mid-twenties now; it's been years since I've seen him. My first thought: Seth looks like his mother with a dark beard glued onto her face. Taking another look, I can make out echoes in the bone: his mother's and maternal grandmother's round heads and neat features replicated, and his great-grandmother's too—I met Hedwig a few times years ago, when she and her husband Rudolf were living in Forest Hills, or visiting us here. And now I think I can make out less striking hints from the Hadas side of the family: the same high forehead and sharp eyes behind thick glasses as Debbie's father—Seth's grandfather—David. These same Davidisms are strongly apparent in Debbie's brother Edward's youngest son, Julian Hadas.

Thomas Hardy's poem "Heredity" nails it:

> I am the family face;
> Flesh perishes, I live on,
> Projecting trait and trace
> Through time to times anon,
> And leaping from place to place

Over oblivion.

The years-heired feature that can
In curve and voice and eye
Despise the human span
Of durance—that is I;
The eternal thing in man
That heeds no call to die.

Bone structure, names, dates; who outside the family, or even inside it, would care?

Especially in the second half of life, simply to live one's life takes much of what most people have to give of energy and curiosity. To trace the ramifying filigree, cat's cradle, spiral, DNA, kinship stretching back how many generations, resemblances that briefly surface in a smile or a gesture or the molding of a skull—no one can be attentive to it all.

I'm not a historian, tracing narrative trails backward, nor an archivist, poring over data I've laboriously uncovered. I respect the eager and patient scholars sifting through the multitudinous past, trying to find the answers to questions I haven't even thought of asking. My energy and curiosity often flag. But it can happen now and then that I'm visited by an unpredictable intimation, some serendipitous connection that snags my attention as it floats my way, say as I'm sitting out on the lawn with Debbie, peering at her phone.

And poetry? That vast and tiny span whose rhythm of hover, dart, soar, return to where the lyric impulse maybe started from—a poem, unpredictable as air, can suddenly sketch out a path that leads who knows where, a train of thought, except that thought is the wrong word, that will arrive where no one can know, least of all the poet writing now.

Proleptic

I fly, says elegy. *I spread my wings.* It has been waiting in the wings. It is the wings. What is it?

Easy to think of as a great white bird, such consolation belongs to flying, the steering through bright air toward a destination. Let the process continue to soar; may no dread vertical pierce us, spear us, stab us, bring us down.

Swoop, says elegy. *I dive. I drop.*

Vernal

The beating of unseen wings got louder. Why? I couldn't guess. Maybe the season spiraling toward blinding green? Fluttering intimations, bird or pulse, hole in the heart or blank space in the brain, trellised over with tenacious new shoots, delicate tracery of each silver vein. Fresh old flavor of survival. Bath of warm spring rain.

The Present Moment: Drawing Lessons

As instructed by the drawing teacher at the Fairbanks Museum, I'm keeping a journal of sketches from nature. And I have the impulse to give this fat little sketchbook a name. It would be easy to say that the theme of such a journal is *The Present Moment.* But since every leaf and twig, every web and blade and drop obeys an imperative in force for millions of years, this has to be—doesn't it?—a heightened present, a moment that stands for much more than itself. Pausing to draw however swift, economical, even minimal a line gives the illusion of arresting time even as it actually consumes a touch of time. We're always playing catch-up; the lines I draw can capture, at most, at best, the profile of the present moment just as it starts to pupate into future.

The Lost Pen

The prophetess in her dark cave intoned: How could I have failed to notice that order is an illusion? Love's bubbling is part of the chaos. To find oneself enmeshed in family, the tangled web of lives, the thread pulled tight: both our birthright and our fated pattern, random, comforting, predictable, hopeless. Past or future? Patch it. Until the next revision, make it new.

I've lost my favorite pen.

We stumble into the story in the middle. Lit by the candle of a complicated hope, the stew of trouble simmers. Barely lidded chaos knocks against the cover of the caldron.

Moonlight on snow: escape from day to dark. Frozen landscape. Acreage for sale: what I thought was mine is under threat, not for the first time—it only feels like the first time. A force field over which clouds drift until the next transformation: incessant billowing, shrinkage, adjustment, revision.

Perhaps the pen has rolled under the table.

Close to the end—the end of what? Whose end? An acolyte waits in the starlight. I could catch planes on time, but where was I going? The time to pay the debt was running out. Art off the walls! Let light have room to frolic. Camel, weasel, whale, and the sky changes: endless variations and replacement among the clouds—pillows for sleep and for unadorned, unpatterned dreams, as if there were such a thing.

I never found that pen, but I picked up another—as if (another as if!) writing it all down—*all* down, impossible—could make a difference. Middle, beginning, end—all out of order.

Sometimes love works like that.

Shirley's Painting

In the painting of a landscape not too far from here, over where Caledonia County becomes Orleans County: red barn, dirt road, steeple in the distance, pointing up from between two hills, familiar, easy to recognize variations on a theme. The tall blue lollipops I think are trees.

Pale sky, cloud cover, no sun. Or maybe the painter wasn't sure how to drape these hills with diffuse wintry light, how to capture the distant dull shimmer of a pond. Notional shimmer only—no coruscation, no ripples breaking up and giving back the light.

Without these lollipop trees—they might be flowers in a giant's garden—the painting would be simply a semi-primitive landscape making confident use of primary colors.

But the looming verticals somehow endow it with a monumentality both somber and surreal. They also skew the human scale. Although come to think of it, there are no human figures in this landscape as rendered by Shirley, in her eighties, looking out over a vista near Barton. From behind her easel on the porch, she could survey it all: steeple, pond, hills, the quiet cloak of a sunless afternoon when anything might happen.

Walk Outside and Back: The Winter Would

A black butterfly is hovering over the winter desk. It's hard to hear the dead voices; it's also a struggle not to listen for them. It was as if nothing seemed to speak, yet everything spoke.

Interpreters lurk behind the trees like sentries, pricking up their ears when I take a short walk to get out of my head. They aren't animals, they're animas. They aren't unfriendly. They seem to know that I'll find them, and that if I have the wherewithal, I'll feed them. But we do not need to speak.

Leap of a deer in the brush. Anonymous track of some light-footed quadruped on snow. Someone just passed me, a poet wearing a grey fur hat, walking fast in the opposite direction.

Reams of pages written by previous occupants fill every room; fill my room, now I'm back inside. Soon after Proust died, Andre Gide dreamed that he entered the library of his late acquaintance and pulled all the books from the shelves.

Cautious in the stillness, Penelope pulled one more all-nighter, unravelling what she had woven the day before.

A black butterfly in the dead of winter? *Time?* says the echo. *Time is not my friend.*

Orchard, Medallions, Owl

I dreamed that we were walking, he and I, through an autumnal orchard. The trees were bare. Instead of leaves, what hung from the branches were countless ceramic medallions, small and round like coins, each stamped with its individual design, each as different as a snowflake from all the others. Terra cotta-colored but also somehow luminous, they chinked and twinkled in the low sunlight.

As if these little medallions were Christmas ornaments on display at a local craft fair, "Who made these?" I asked. Someone replied that one old woman in the neighborhood had made them all by hand. I knew without being told that these objects were not for sale.

We now reached a place where the trees started to thin out—not only apple trees, it now appeared, but maples and birches and pines. On a high branch of one tall tree, an enormous owl was perching. As we stood back to get a better view, it opened its wings and launched itself into a sky that now was blazing blue. It soared and sailed away.

This was a dawn dream. It took me all morning and well into the afternoon of that long sleepy day (not an autumn day at all but a day at the start of summer), a day of downpour, drizzle, intermittent sun, repeat, to anatomize my dream as best I could. Any attempt to parse a dream is not only incomplete, it's doomed. Who can remember their dream, let alone understand it? It took those slow uncrowded hours, and a noon nap in the raftered attic, rain drumming on the roof a little while, the only other sound the mild wheezing of the cat asleep on a chair at the foot of the bed—it took that long to understand that those dream medallions hanging from the tree, all with a family resemblance but also all different, were poems. Were my poems. I was the local old woman who had made them all by hand and then had carefully hung them, one by one, on the deciduous trees of the imagination in their autumnal grove. "Home-made! But aren't we all?" asks Robinson Crusoe in Elizabeth Bishop's poem "Crusoe in England." Like Crusoe's umbrella or his flute or his home-brew, isn't most art still home-made? Even in the age of AI, mine certainly is.

I had originally thought I'd been one of the spectators who watched the owl take flight and vanish into the empyrean. Was it the owl of wisdom, of inspiration, flying out of sight? But perhaps I'd also been the owl.

All that misty afternoon and on into the evening, as the rain let up and started again, let up and started again, now soft, now loud, all afternoon and evening, in the absence of distractions, I became more and more aware of a grateful astonishment, an unexpected and startling gratitude, that once I sensed its presence not only persisted but spread. Gratitude for what surrounded me, for where I found myself. There was the big attic, its corners piled with boxes whose ripe, half-forgotten contents promised to yield surprises. There was the bed I kept returning to, its faded quilt, the cats coming and going, now on a chair, now in the cat loft, now curled up between my beloved and me. The old house, the rain, the seasons, the years, the time, the memories. Past summers came and went like the rain, now tempestuous, now gentle as a mist.

Gratitude, too, for those little medallions. Gifts no one had asked for, gifts carefully crafted by some undisclosed process and hung in the trees for whoever might pass by to examine and define. And that great owl, flying away, leaving a track in the mind. Gratitude for the whole improbable—what to call it? That in-between-ness, that both and -ness, that porch of the imagination where inside and outside meet, those leafless trees with their home-made harvest.

Black and White: Suspension Bridge

Peering at the page, I squint at what goes bumptious and boldface even as I try to set it down in black on white. Are these all lies, twinkling among the lines I make as I write?

Whatever it is that I'm trying to seal under the surface beats its wings, frantic to escape from the prison of either eye. One eye blinks *tell*, the other winks *distill*. Reach out, Tell says. Build a suspension bridge of narrative experience can cross, finger-walking its hand along the railing. The listener meets the teller in the middle, ending where the other one began. Under the bridge, far below, a river is running.

All this is known already, says Distill, so you can leave most of it out. Delete. Compress. Transform.

The world sways, the bridge trembles. I try to keep writing. Crossing the bridge, leaning into the wind: what dear, dead fingers also touched this page? And this sudden heat—where does it come from? I see: a cauldron of exclusions is simmering somewhere nearby, the humming heat of all that's in the pot, the letters looping and writhing and the panes steamed up. What's cooking? Ellipses, corrections, hiatuses that fill the book of days. Some words bully others. But all of them as I scribble, clauses subordinate yet not yet left out, pulled from oblivion, rescued on the page—they all make marks for someone to decipher. The act of writing fights the drift of white.

Wreath Blown Down

Yellow chrysanthemum petals scattered in front of the fountain: one of three large, elaborate floral wreaths mounted on wire stands has blown over. Like a ribbon across a chest, diagonal across the fallen wreath is a crumpled satin sash with EMS spelled out in glittery letters. We hoist the wreath and set it back up on its tripod's flimsy feet. Not that the wreath is heavy, but neither is it stable. Its two companion wreaths are still standing, but for how long? A chilly wind is blowing. Soon the sun will sink into the river.

These three wreaths stood, when all of them were still standing, in front of the fountain which is the focal point of the Firemen's Monument. On either side of the fountain sits a massive, sculptured figure, eloquent in the silent idiom of stone. There is a language not of flowers or wreaths or ribbons only. The petals fallen from the wreath, the solidity of the matching statues: their dialects vary, their message is the same. They all push back against oblivion.

Paused in their postures, the sculpted figures: on one side of the fountain, a woman cradles a dead fireman in her arms. The woman on the other side holds two children, clearly fatherless children, in her lap. These stone women invite us to mourn along with them. In a more ephemeral mode, the wreaths commemorate what we have all lost. Seasonal, fragile, golden, the flowers serve as timekeepers. Otherwise, time has stopped.

Every part of this scene reaches out, but with tremendous decorum, reticence, control. Everything is eloquent without the need for speech—no speech now and none then, when the fountain and its sculptures were put in place more than a century ago.

9/11 was a long day. Late that afternoon I went to the park—and I was not alone—to sit on one of the benches that flanked and still flank the monument. Earlier that afternoon, the fountain's deep, wide basin, empty of water except in summer, had held one flower—as I remember, a yellow rose. By nightfall the basin was brimming over with bouquets. Three hundred forty-three New York City firemen, it was known by then, had died that morning.

As the days and weeks went by, people often lit small candles and placed them carefully on the fountain's rim. The candles burned out and were replaced. Drops of wax made tracks along the brickwork in front of the fountain. If one were to follow these drops, as Hansel and Gretel followed the trail of breadcrumbs in to the dark forest, where might they lead?

The seasons came and went, and then the years. The sun sank into the river, a little further south as each winter came. The moon waxed and waned. Twenty years went by at a stately pace—or, scattered like golden petals over the stone, they vanished in a flash.

And now? The toppled wreath which, before we righted it, might have been expected to look absurd, as awkward as a suddenly glimpsed undergarment no one is supposed to see, has managed on the contrary to retain its dignity. It had fallen down? So it had fallen down. To be deciduous must have been part of the process; part of the grammar governing the ineluctable verb *to change.* The little yellow petals were scattered over the bricks on either side, more durable than flesh if less solid than granite; the human gestures, the push against oblivion, in an unwritten language all of us can read.

The Requirement

I thought I was tired of poetry—weary, dry, wrung out, or else overfilled, saturated. Possibly even both. The space that should have been devoted to poetry was frozen blank or stuffed with chores and fears. When had this happened? It must have been gradual. There had been no liminal moment when I said goodbye to poetry, or poetry said goodbye to me.

Not a total goodbye, of course. Last week I had the impulse to welcome back the hummingbirds. What better than poetry to celebrate the occasion of their reappearance?

And immediately a lattice-work of possible patterns began its habitual silent, semi-conscious weaving: a villanelle, maybe. And rhymes suggested themselves: bird, heard, word. Return, burn, learn, churn. (Gilbert and Sullivan: "Girl, do you ever yearn?" "I yearn my living."). That went nowhere. The pattern dangled, waiting without enthusiasm to be finished. I let it hang there in midair. The poem could wait; or more likely, it would never be finished.

And yet.

Yesterday, a hundred people or more sat in a big white tent. Through a narrow slit between two tent flaps, the blazing July afternoon outside was a portal to another world almost within reach. But while the flowery meadow out there burned in sunlight, we in the audience all seemed content to stay where we were and listen.

To listen to poetry again: breaking through a sticky web and moving toward a big closed chest that had been waiting somewhere out of sight. The chest wasn't locked, it was simply stuck; it hadn't been opened in a while. But the sound of voices reading poems acted like a lubricant, and it turned out to be easy to lift the lid. Inside, the chest was packed, full to the brim, with colorful layers of softly folded silks: salmon, chartreuse, gold, scarlet, azure scarves tenderly laid down and fitted in—a dowry of the imagination, stored and preserved and then forgotten until our gathered presence this summer Sunday afternoon functioned like an Open Sesame, and there were the colors and textures, the deliciousness, unspoiled, fresh, waiting.

The first spring of the pandemic, we came up here early in April. Every other day, it seemed to snow: snow, sun, melt, repeat. And when we first ventured upstairs to the freezing cold, uninsulated attic, a surprise: mice or squirrels or chipmunks turned out to have been busy in the winter. The rafters were festooned, looped with silk scarves, fuchsia, turquoise, salmon, apple green, all twisted around some upper beams so tightly that a vigorous tug couldn't dislodge them. These small creatures had brought my scarves, left hanging on pegs in the bedroom, into the attic—but wait, the attic door was closed all winter. They must have had their own secret pathways in the roof and walls.

There was no reason to pull down these unexpected streamers, at least not right away. They looked so festive, and they were so mysterious. Who would have thought that these invisible interior decorators could have been so busy through the cold, dark months? But why not? They had been busy, and here was the proof, and the proof was a gift. The scarves hung like banners from the high ceiling of a deserted banquet hall that might now again begin to welcome guests to the feast.

I had forgotten the shock, the silent celebration of these silken colors. But now, more than two years later, in the white tent, as we all heard the readers' voices and felt the heat of the sun through the white roof of the tent, as, mostly unmasked, we breathed in whatever dangerous particles were floating in the warm air, we also sensed the shimmer of recovered memories. I'm certain that I was not alone in reexamining the bottomless resources of—the mind? The memory? The senses? The capacity for delight? I know that we paid close attention as Sharon Olds, her hands shaking, her spirit ebullient, her voice at once mischievous and urgent, reminded her listeners, "So much pleasure is required of us." And we rose to the requirement.

How to assimilate joy? Consider the obstacles; disbelief that it's real; fear that it will vanish; jealous protection of this new zone of privacy, this treasure that (is it selfish to say?) is ours, yours and mine, and no one else's? But gradually the tightly folded bud opens out like that old chest in the attic, and reveals a glass of blessings, as George Herbert's poem "The Pulley" has it. Or to change the trope: do we count, or do we superstitiously not count, these golden fruits heavy with fragrant promise, hanging from a tree whose name we know? Shepherds in Samos in the Seventies didn't like to be asked how many goats were in their flock. Bad luck to admire one, to point, to count. Can we reach up and pick the fruit, overcome hesitation and fear and enter into bliss, senses slowed and trembling, eyes, mouths, hands all tenderly exploring regions almost beyond the reach of memory in both our lives until now? Can we? We have, we do.

Behind shut eyes, a blaze of light: the body, lying back, bathing in a tank of water spangled with stars, wakes without instruction to a world it recognizes as reborn. And oscillation: whether standing still or lying down, we are rocked gently to and fro.

Waves of silence rise and fall around the little boat in which, my fellow voyager, we have set sail together, starting in icebound winter waters through days and weeks, a melt of hope and fear, and always the warm current of longing sweeping us toward an arrival which is also a beginning, so that we've both passed and keep on passing through a paradisiacal portal streaming with nameless light.

Separate pasts, two lives that joined up late: in marrying each other we ventured through a gate into a world the same shape as before, but lit with a new glow. What had I been running toward, running away from, those years before? Where had I been scurrying in such a hurry? With you I could stand still. I wanted to be nowhere else but here. I could sit and listen to poetry, or venture up the stairs and come upon the silk banners in the attic. There was so much to discover and to recover. And there was plenty, if not to forget, then to store in a chest that might one day be opened.

In you I married compassion and protection and distress, generosity and tenderness beyond what I had known or could imagine. In you I married light and dark, buoyancy and weight.

Not that standing still, or lying back in a tank of water that reflects the stars, or sailing on and on in our little boat, will last forever. Age and death step into every green meadow, every cold attic, every sun-soaked tent. Our sanctuary, every sanctuary, balances on the edge of a precipice. Everyone in the tent that Sunday knew it; joy was required of us all the same. On the verge, on the ledge, we hold onto one another.

Sun and Ice

Sun glints off ice; etches each line in a beloved face, and strokes a finger over scanty snow under a leafless tree, so that what looked drab a blink ago now ignites with radiance. Dusk does arrive, and soon, but not before a fleeting, tender light softens the brown and white earth with a rosy pink, like a promise.

The days are getting longer; it's the years that speed by. One Sunday that first February, "Let's get some air," you said. Was it early in the afternoon? We took a walk in the park; the river was pocked with broken ice. When we'd gotten chilly enough to turn around and head back, it was as if the season tilted: suddenly lavish sun was pouring through the bedroom window, lighting up the threadbare red sheets, warming our bodies with the help of the hot radiator hissing *now* and *now*, even as now is then.

The Scarlet Arrow

Not a dream; it only reads that way.

I never trusted spring. My mode, I always thought, was bleaker, autumnal, forever looking back over its shoulder. But elegy gets tired. As we all do, it ages.

I turn my face to April. The vernal version reenacts itself each year; with a tender gesture, it strews new over old, offers a green greeting, waves to withered leaves gleaming in new light.

I'm standing blinking in a doorway, poised between inside and out. Just outside the door, if I were to step out, on a whitewashed wall, a bright red arrow is pointing. Which way? On a radiant blank page, on a turned-down sheet, in a garden bed, that semaphore in red.

Misery? Bliss? It isn't spring or fall. It's early and it's late. Why do I say I'm poised between inside and outside, when you and I have already gone through a gate?

Dream: Silver and Gold

I had a dream the other night of going back to the island, silvery streets parallel to the shoreline. It was a dream of the third act, a return journey to a place one has loved and lived in and left and lost and then come briefly back to. A gull swooped. A wet stone gleamed on the path.

I took a train last week north through a short November afternoon to a place I hadn't been in years. The houses and the stations, all like something in an Edward Hopper painting, glowed in the late sun, aa solid and immoveable as if not one brick could ever budge. It was a vision of borrowed time repaid with golden interest. The sunset-gilded Sound, the long unspooling ribbon of the track—nothing had aged or changed except for me.

September Sun

The sun: a blade slicing across the floor. A pool in which the cat basks on a tabletop. A slat of brightness further fading the faded quilt. A smear, a spill, a veil, honey drizzled over the afternoon, drape slowly mantling a slope of green. Blackberries ripen. Apples hang; fall. The days are getting shorter. The sun: a blade you want to graze your skin.

The Amphitheater

Steep grassy hill that slopes down to an amphitheater distant as the bottom of a well: a memory from Greece. Here in the north country, it's September: last concert in the summer series over at Dog Mountain. Before the pandemic, these concerts were every other week, but this post-pandemic summer they're weekly, as if to fit in everything we've missed.

Scratch out *post.* In the perpetual middle of a wave that never crests but builds, subsides, builds again, we're dancing this afternoon on a steep incline, *we* being diapered toddlers, octogenarians, and everything in between, dancing with such abandon that one old man slips and falls. And gets right back up and goes on dancing. Old man? Say my age.

As the near recedes, or even if it doesn't recede, things further back come limping into focus, piecemeal, unpredictable. Today, for example, for whatever reason—well, surely the steep slope of Dog Mountain has something to do with it—I am transported to two less than successful attempts at sleep, both from the nineteen seventies in Greece. First, a non-nap in Naxos: blood-gorged mosquitoes squished against a white, or no longer white, stucco wall behind the bed. And then a hillside dotted with thorny shrubs, somewhere outside Olympia. We were sleeping outdoors—why? It was getting light when some bug flew into my nose and out again, and the sun rose, and it was 1974, a date fished from oblivion by the hook of history. Cyprus has been invaded.

Precarious slopes where dancers trip and fall and right themselves again, while the music plays on. Earthquake pandemic Haiti Afghanistan. That was a few years ago; now a new set of emergencies crowd the headlines, which doesn't mean that the other emergencies have gone away. There is room, as I wrote earlier in a purely personal context, for only so much attention.

The sun sets behind Dog Mountain earlier each Sunday afternoon.

Storing the Season

The problem is the prodigality: apples and blackberries in profusion, both fruits by their respective natures hard to reach. Tangle of brambles, berries glossy black: even to graze them with a fingertip, you have to stretch over a jungle of thorny vines and balance on a rotting log. Rosy apples cluster like the bride in Sappho at the tip of a branch too high to reach.

Too much. Go for what can be eaten. Berry a bucketful and cook into jam. Or apples: slice, boil, strain into warm sauce. Inhale the rising steam, fragrant distillation of, and at, the end of summer.

The summer offers other harvests too, less tangible, harder to preserve. What to do with misty mornings burning off to blue? With spangled spider webs that delicately stitch two blades of grass together? You can't consume a sight. Or what about that lichened rock on which I used to perch and gaze out at the lines of drying hay striping the field?

Is it possible to take all these away with me, to pack and then unpack them, arrange them, spread them out like presents on a bed? Gifts—for whom? For everyone. And the occasion? No occasion. The rending gold of summer ending—I can only try to fold it into poetry.

Applesauce

By the end of August I'm spending less time on the porch and more time prowling around the periphery, where the grass gets long except for flat patches where the deer have lain. It's apple season—time to make applesauce. I fill jars with the stuff and give most of it away to friends and neighbors.

It's a multi-stage process: pick up mostly windfalls, most of which are Duchess apples from our heroically prolific old tree, but also a few flinty Wolf Rivers and some smaller, rosy-golden apples from under the tree at the side of Library Road, where the Danville and St. Johnsbury town lines meet. Then there are the slightly pear-shaped greenish pale apples from near Barb Machell's driveway, or snow-white globes—both skin and flesh as white as balls of cotton—from one of the trees our nearest neighbors the O'Briens planted. At least when it comes to applesauce, diversity-equity-inclusion works: the more different varieties are boiled down together, the tangier and tastier the result.

Cut the apples up—I generally use a rather dull old cleaver—into reasonable-sized pieces, maybe about six or eight per apple depending on the size, leaving skin and seeds and core and stem. Boil in a big pot—enamel is good—with plenty of water. Whatever juice boils over will smell delicious but will stick to your stove top. When the texture of the apple slices is unformly soft, let cool and then, a crucial step, but all steps are crucial, strain: I use my invaluable old Foley Food Mill. The resulting detritus, slick with apple skins, tastes good but will go on the compost heap. What's left when all the seeds/skin/stem parts have been strained out should be tart.

Once I'm back in the city, buying even a variety of apples from the farmers' market, the resulting sauce tastes sweet and bland.

Back up here, the sauce will need some maple syrup, and of course cinnamon, cloves, and nutmeg to taste—a shortcut is ready-mixed apple or pumpkin pie spice—and maybe some brown sugar. Better to sweeten too little than too much; you can always add syrup later. Pour into sterilized jars and give away, saving enough to eat at home. I like applesauce warmed up, with a little milk added, and maybe a drizzle more maple syrup.

The other morning, something stung me. A wasp or yellow-jacket had drilled its way into a Duchess apple that was nestling half concealed in the tall tangle of dew-wet grass and ferns under the tree. I heedlessly reached down; and whatever was sucking apple juice the stem end of the fruit let me know that my groping hand wasn't welcome. Cold; wet; the satisfying round shapes you have to feel for blindly down there in the grass; the sudden pain. This is my apple, said the yellow-jacket. The deer or raccoons leave apple cores with nibble marks, but don't stick around to dispute their territory.

Every day these waning weeks of summer, I feel impelled to gather as many rosy globes as I can fit into the stained and fragrant canvas bag devoted to the purpose. It might hold a dozen apples or more, though at the height of the season in a good year, the Duchess tree drops more like twenty or thirty apples every day. I feel impelled to take home what cannot be taken: the flavor of memory, the memory of fragrance. To take home time. And if I can take this intangible home, I should also be able to distribute it.

Each apple is both end product and embryo, rich with seeds, full of promise: "So careful of the type she seems,/So careless of the single life," wrote Tennyson of nature in *In Memoriam.* Each apple is also a sweet synecdoche, a condensation of many apples, a distillation of past summers. The past falls from the tree; the future falls from the tree. Which will I touch, in my blind groping around in the grass underfoot? Or will I be stung before I can put the apple in my bag?

By noon, now in mid-September, tall shadows are already looming, dark and melodramatic, striping the lawn and garden. Friendly ghosts remain, but most of the guests have receded, each taking with them a jar of applesauce to taste or inhale and remember. Or to give away. Emptier, the house seems both bigger and smaller. A cycle fills with stillness. Silence grows on the trees. These last mornings I put on the rubber boots I bought at Morrison's Feed Bag, the crimson boots imprinted with yellow chickens, and head out across the cold wet spiderweb-spangled grass toward the Duchess tree. "May something always go unharvested," wrote Robert Frost. Almost everything goes unharvested. I pick an apple up and take a bite.

The Author

Rachel Hadas's recent books include *Love and Dread*, *Pandemic Almanac*, and *Ghost Guest*. Her translations include Euripides's Iphigenia plays and a portion of Nonnus's *Tales of Dionysus*. Professor Emerita at Rutgers-Newark, where she taught for many years, she now teaches at 92Y in New York City and serves as poetry editor of *Classical Outlook*. Her honors include a Guggenheim fellowship and an award from the American Academy-Institute of Arts and Letters.

www.ingramcontent.com/pod-product-compliance
Lightning Source LLC
Chambersburg PA
CBHW030428310726
48979CB00009B/1665/J

9781939574398